WHAT PEOPLE ARE SAYING ABOUT

SELF ENQUIRY: ON BEING YOU.
A JOURNEY INTO TRUTH

In his book *A Journey into Truth*, Michael Vincent shares the powerful tool of Self Enquiry with seasoned clarity and precision. Whether you are new to the process of introspection or already on the path of enquiry you will find support, nourishment and value here. Complementing an explanation of the process with his beautiful and unique artwork Michael gently, firmly and repeatedly guides you towards the living Truth of the Self. The direct experience of the S ⁃ is Existence-Consciousness-Bliss and this book will be ⸱ ⸱enefit in recognizing, realizing and actualizing this.
JM Harrison, Author, *Naked Being*

In this lovely book Michael skilf ⸱ y. He reconnects us to and reminds us of ⸱ ack Kerouac once poetically described th ⸱ easure as the "Golden Entity". Michael is a ⸱ ⸱h-seeker whose journeying is authentic. He walks firm⸱ ⸱nd the talk with his simple, profound and yet elusive message of Truth, Love and Light found throughout these pages. Highly recommended, *A Journey into Truth* is a generous open call to Spirit.
Mark Pogson, Founder Magpie Qigong, Advanced Tai Chi Instructor and Shiatsu Practitioner

Michael's book is profound, reminding me in a direct way of what has always been there. His book is verbiage-free and has a rawness which I find very refreshing reminding me that connecting to one's inner self is not about adding on but about de-layering and letting go. Whether you are a beginner on your road to finding your Truth and need a good map, or a well-travelled soul that just needs a little reminding, I thoroughly recommend Michael's book. It is direct, easy to comprehend and an essential tool to connect you to your Truth and source of Being. **Linda Byrne**, Founder and Director LVB Dance; Self Enquiry devotee

For me Self Enquiry is an absolute cornerstone of any spiritual pathway. So many people seem to pass it by flocking to dance workshops or Tantra seeking connection. But Self Enquiry is the royal route to the centre of Being and I think it is wonderful that Michael has written this easy-to-read guide. I hope it inspires many more people to engage in this important Practice. **Devaraj Sandberg**, Director, Osho Leela, Gillingham, Dorset

Thank you for writing this book. It comes at a time when I am being challenged more than ever by my unconscious and conditioned thoughts as I continue to delve deeper inwardly to uproot the unreal and rediscover the True. Your words serve as a simple, clear and powerful reminder yet again that to recognize who I really am means nothing more than commitment to the question "Who Am I?" and looking closely at what arises is required. I know this line of Self Enquiry to be authentic and may your book be read by all who are drawn to this Practice. **Christopher Pogioli**, Dedicated Self Enquirer

Self Enquiry:
On Being You

A Journey into Truth

Self Enquiry:
On Being You

A Journey into Truth

Michael Vincent

BOOKS

Winchester, UK
Washington, USA

First published by O-Books, 2016
O-Books is an imprint of John Hunt Publishing Ltd., Laurel House, Station Approach,
Alresford, Hants, SO24 9JH, UK
office1@jhpbooks.net
www.johnhuntpublishing.com

For distributor details and how to order please visit the 'Ordering' section on our website.

Text copyright: Michael Vincent 2015

ISBN: 978 1 78535 273 7
Library of Congress Control Number: 2015949726

A CIP catalogue record for this book is available from the British Library.

Design: Lee Nash

Printed in the USA by Edwards Brothers Malloy

We operate a distinctive and ethical publishing philosophy in all
areas of our business, from our global network of authors to
production and worldwide distribution.

CONTENTS

1. Introduction   1
2. Historical Perspective: There is nothing new in this...   9
3. The place of personal experience in Self Enquiry   16
4. The Practice: "Nan Yar: Who Am I?"   22
5. Step 1: I am not that...   27
6. Step 2: Limitation is of the mind   32
7. Step 3: Unlearning the learned   41
8. Step 4: Relinquish Desire   47
9. Step 5: Feeling and Emotion   51
10. Step 6: Conscience, action and behaviour   56
11. Step 7: Be in your body but not of it   62
12. Step 8: Earth Matters   67
13. Step 9: On Unity   74
14. Step 10: Be free   79
15. Step 11: I Am This...   84

Recommended Reading   90
Notes   91
Illustrations   94
About the Author   95
Previous Books   98

Author's Note

I am delighted to publish this book in O-Books' "Made Easy" range of titles. It is my hope that Self Enquiry will now become more accessible to a wider readership and the growing number of seekers ready to follow this simple yet profound Practice. My intention in writing this book is to make the map of the journey clearer for you, to provide you with a guidebook so to speak for a personal journey you must make to discover whatever awaits you.

In a world confronted with social, political and environmental upheaval on an unprecedented scale, the journey into Truth is potentially more challenging than it has ever been and at the same time never more important.

"Of many thousand mortals, one, perchance,
Striveth for Truth; and of those few that strive –
Nay, and rise high – one only – here and there –
Knoweth me, as I am, the very Truth."
Bhagavad-Gita
The Song Celestial

This book is dedicated to all who have shared Satsang with me as we make the journey into Truth, the Truth for all of us to find as we focus inwards, in silence, expecting nothing but welcoming whatever arises.

With special thanks to:

Linda Byrne, Hilary Lepine, Jonathan Harrison, Christopher Pogioli, Jon Pogioli, John Emery, Mark Pogson, Stephen Gawtry (Watkins' *Mind Body Spirit Magazine*), Claire Gillman (*Kindred Spirit* Magazine), Devaraj Sandberg (Director, Osho Leela, Gillingham)

Michael Vincent
AshTat,
Bridgwater, Somerset
2015

1

Introduction

You came into your body with nothing: without your name, your mind, your ego, your personality and without any material thing. It is assured you will leave your body with nothing. What is the nature of this "I" before these things were attached to it?

"Nan Yar – Who Am I?"

I suspect since humankind first developed an awareness of a spiritual dimension to existence Self Enquiry in some form has been practised. Indeed Self Enquiry is an ancient Practice embraced by the major religions and one which has inspired many figures in world history: politicians, spiritual leaders, composers, artists, writers, philosophers and scientists. Why am I here? What is my purpose? Why do I exist? "Who Am I?"

In the mind-centred West this simple but radical Practice has become enmeshed in verbiage, notably over the last 100 years into the 21st century. Weighty, complex texts have been written, retreat centres established and many pilgrimages made to sacred places across the globe in the search for answers to these questions, to discover the nature of Truth, whatever that may be. This is often to the detriment of Self Enquiry and its message resulting in confusion and uncertainty for the seeker, the pilgrim, the ordinary man and woman who, in becoming aware that something exists beyond the physical world, is seeking the nature of Truth.

In doing this, in stripping away the flowery language and sweet sugar coating so to speak, I am aware that I am presenting Self Enquiry as the challenging Practice it is designed to be, directly, "in the raw". But then this will take you to an important question: who, or what, is being challenged? What is it within you that creates this resistance, doubt, fear, this seeming mountain that is now before you as you confront full-on the issues presented to you as you proceed with the Practice? This is your first opportunity to go to the source, to step back from this anxiety and concern and see it for what it is: the many-layered mind with all its attachments continuing its gameplaying in its effort to remain in control. In being prepared to swallow what seems to be a bitter pill you are taken directly to what matters: the path to Truth.

My first book on Self Enquiry, completed in 2010 during my stay at Sri Ramana's Ashram in Arunachala, India, sought to clarify the nature of Self Enquiry, to free it from spiritual jargon and flowery language and make this important Practice accessible to those who are ready for it. Since that time I have continued to lead Satsang* and Retreats focusing on Self Enquiry and have worked to clarify for myself just how this Practice can be "taught" to others and made even clearer and more accessible for everyone. This book, in growing from the first, addresses these questions and seeks to further clarify a Practice that is, essentially, so very simple and so very profound.

The first thing to understand is this: Self Enquiry is not an intellectual exercise presenting you with a "problem" for your mind to sort out so it can give you an answer. In becoming that its purpose, to take you beyond mind into stillness, is defeated. The mind's ability to find such an answer is beyond its capability anyway. The Practice is grounded on experience not intellectual analysis, and its application centres on your personal experience as life is lived in your physical body. I have long understood this to be the case. My life since childhood has given me ample opportunity to test this, to experience for myself how it works as I apply the Practice to the challenges I have faced, and continue to.

So let us be clear from the beginning. Books and texts may

serve a purpose as signposts, pointers and maps for you the seeker on a personal journey; or they may be of no use to you whatsoever. Let us be clear on this too: reading these texts and attending retreats are not required "qualifications" in preparing you to proceed with the Practice. Such texts are potentially useful maps; the gurus** and teachers you may meet on your journey are simply guides and helping hands. When no longer needed by the seeker, when the journey is known and understood, both teachers and texts are set aside, lovingly and with thanks. The Truth, whatever that might be, is for you to find as you focus inwards learning from the lessons of life as it is lived, the true purpose of Self Enquiry.

It is with this understanding that this present volume is written. It consists of a series of reflections and observations made during periods of personal meditation and my work with those who have participated in Satsang. In essence these pages are a description of the journey we share together, in Truth. Some are answers to questions asked during Satsang, others are reflections on observations made during personal periods of meditation written with the intention, humbly, that they may be of service to others. The journey we share can be seen as a number of steps taken by the traveller at whatever pace and speed is required. There is no hurry, no pressure, no agenda other than to reach journey's end whenever and wherever that may be.

It is a journey that will sometimes be hard going as you relinquish the accumulated layers and baggage, the stuff that has created the false identities in which you have believed for so long. This is the fog that obscures the path on which you walk already. As your journey continues you come to understand that this accumulated garbage is mind-created illusion. The only place it exists is in your mind. The travelling will become easier for you as each layer you relinquish, each bit of baggage you set down, each cloud that shifts makes the next step lighter giving

3

you more energy to proceed.

If it helps you there are ways you can visualise your journey. With each step you take imagine yourself throwing off another layer of unwanted clothing; you can see yourself on a train, and instead of carrying your baggage on your back set it down or, better still, throw it out the window! Visualise the fog lifting, the clouds clearing and with dawning awareness the sun rising and shining. Remember too that setting out on your journey without total commitment is like getting on the train and insisting you carry your baggage or getting off the train before reaching your destination. Enter fully into the Practice with total openness, with no expectations of the outcome and with the intention of getting to your destination however long it may take and no matter how challenging the journey may be.

Finally I would like to make this important observation. Self Enquiry has the potential to help you confront and resolve all personal issues no matter how painful, deeply-ingrained and long-term they may be. Held in your mind these are the obstacles obscuring your path to understanding the nature of True Self. Self Enquiry cannot change your past or delete things you wished never happened to you, but it will change your perception of these often painful experiences. I became aware of this profound lesson with my beloved wife Kaisa as we shared her understanding that unresolved and long-held emotional issues were the root cause of her cancer. These issues centred around her childhood as a refugee in Finland after her family's eviction by the Russians from their Karelian homeland. All members of the family, including my beloved wife, carried throughout their lives a deeply-held conviction that they were social outcasts unloved and unwelcome in their own country. Kaisa acknowledged it was too late for her to resolve this issue within herself. Her cancer had progressed beyond the point of healing. But it was not too late for me. This understanding was such a great gift carrying a powerful message for me and one I wish to share with you.

Unresolved issues like this fester away over time, becoming anger, rage and resentment burning within you. It comes as no surprise, on reflection, that such deep-held emotions carried over so many years are a fertile seedbed for cancer and other life-threatening diseases.

Self Enquiry cannot alter or eradicate your past but it will provide you with the tools and the ability to change your perception of it, to rid yourself of this baggage carried within your mind for so long, bringing peace and healing into your life. In freeing yourself from this deep-seated accumulated garbage it will no longer be an obstacle on your path to Self Realisation. In this process Self Enquiry goes deeper in healing your pain than any pill from any bottle. Drugs may bring you temporary relief but once their effect has worn off the pain is likely to return. Self Enquiry, in going to the source, the very root of your suffering, brings about a permanent change in your perception and under-standing of your pain, its cause and its resolution. The simple fact is a bucketful of painkillers will not end a pain the source and cause of which remains unresolved. The peace that Self Enquiry brings into your life and the healing which follows will ease such pain with the potential to end it, permanently.

What is Truth? The answer is for you to discover for yourself.

* * *

Included within the text are reproductions of my paintings of our precious Mother Earth which, in sustaining all that lives, so often clarifies and illuminates issues and problems for us. I remember as a child reading John Clare's wonderful words:

Where the flowers are, God is and I am free...

As questions arise and observations are made whilst you read this book I invite you to go for a walk by the sea, into a wood, contemplate the beauty of a single flower whilst listening to birdsong, feeling the sun on your face or the wind on your skin. Greater clarity, understanding, calmness and peace simply arise from within you, naturally. The paintings in this book are my records of such times spent in nature, close to the Earth, resolving within myself the issues that will arise for you as you read these pages and use the Practice in your everyday life.

* * *

The realisation of True Self, of being who you are, is a personal journey, one you will make alone assisted here and there by a helping hand, a signpost, a guiding light. It is the main act, that which matters. It is a journey we all make at some time in our existence, often when confronted with a crisis or at the point of leaving our bodies. But a journey we will make only when we are ready; and you will know when this is so. The time will come when all that has been learned, from whatever source, will be set aside as you travel inwards in your search for Truth.

Self Enquiry is often described as the direct path to this Truth, the Truth for you to find as you look within in silence and without effort. Self Enquiry is self-sufficiency. You have within you all you require to proceed with the Practice and you are already fully qualified. Trusting that this is so and setting aside all mind-created resistance and doubt is the key that opens the door that is itself an illusion.

This map, this guide, is presented to you with heartfelt love. It is essentially a workbook, a "meditation tool" for you to employ as and when you need and for as long as it is of use to you. The only qualification you require is to be open, expecting nothing whilst being ready for anything that arises. I invite you to commit fully to the journey and when you have finished with the map please pass it to a friend.

Belief is transitory. Truth is constant.
It is for you to find as you look within, effortlessly, asking:

"Nan Yar: Who Am I?"

*Satsang: A Sanskrit word of two parts: "sat" truth and "sang" company. In essence Satsang means a group of people coming together to discuss the nature of Truth.

**Guru is a Sanskrit term for teacher or master.

The beauty of the moon is lost on one whose eyes are closed.

2

Historical Perspective:
There is nothing new in this…

Mahatma Gandhi once said, *"I have nothing new to teach the world. Truth and non-violence are as old as the hills."* The same could be said of Self Enquiry. There is nothing new in what I have to say about this Practice, simply, I humbly suggest, the way in which I intend to say it; and I have nothing to sell you that you do not already possess. This will become clearer as you read this book and the texts recommended to you which are at the heart of Self Enquiry and show the impact this ancient Practice has had throughout history. I will stress, however, that you do not need to read or "understand" these sometimes complex and over-wordy texts in order to qualify to proceed with the Practice. Such reading can be deeply rewarding but is not required; it can give the assurance, should doubt arise, that you are on the right path.

There are many texts from different cultures dating back many centuries up to the present day. In deciding where to begin I have selected a few key texts and teachings which I consider most relevant to the Practice of Self Enquiry.

For a description of the nature of *"The Sovereign Soul"*, the True Self which Self Enquiry seeks to clarify, I will begin with *Bhagavad-Gita, "The Song Celestial"*, described as the prevailing Brahmanic belief of the Hindu religion and written, possibly, around 2000 years ago. It is a key document in Self Enquiry and one I often refer to, sometimes on a daily basis. Throughout its pages this beautiful poem carries a wide-sweeping description of *"The undying Spirit"*, one who is free of desire, ambition, is self-sufficient, honourable and lovingly gives to all without expecting reward. Remaining *"True to the farther Truth"* he *"cannot be stirred or shook by the gravest grief"*, his thoughts are controlled and his passions set aside. These qualities are echoed in the Holy Qur'an which honours patience, firmness and self-control underlining the importance of righteous deeds and compassion.

Self Enquiry embraces Advaita, non-duality and unity. All are one with God and all that lives, often referred to as *"Oneness"*. There is no separation: them and us, enlightened-unenlightened, worthy-unworthy etc. Such categorisation creates division and isolation often resulting in conflict. Jesus Christ makes this clear throughout His teaching:

> *There is neither Jew nor Greek, there is neither bond nor free, there is neither male nor female: for ye are all one in Christ Jesus.*
> *Galatians 3:2*

You are in God and God is in you. There is no separation. This sentiment is echoed by the Sufi Poet Mansur Hallaj when he asked his creator: *"Who are you?"* to be told *"You!"* and in Krishna's words in the Gita: *"I am alike for all! I know not hate, I know not favour... They are in me, and I am in them."* If you wish to see God look in the mirror or into the eyes of another living being.

For *Bhagavad-Gita* one living in Truth loves all that lives treating friend and foe equally, showing love for all; Jesus Christ welcomed all into His fold whilst Allah is... *"full of bounty to all the worlds"*. The Tao Te Ching, first written down in the 1st century BC, expresses a similar sentiment in these words:

> *... see your community in other communities,*
> *Think of countries as part of your being,*
> *And treasure the world as the round centre of everything.*

Love is the undercurrent that flows through these texts, the fundamental quality that unites us all whilst healing all Earth's ills, acknowledged in the Holy Qur'an in the words of Allah when

... He joined your hearts in love...
Surah 3:103

Taking this a little further we find that love and compassion go hand-in-hand with forgiveness throughout these teachings, clearly expressed in Jesus Christ's last words:

Then said Jesus, "Father, forgive them; for they know not what they do."
Luke 23:34

These beautiful words point to a quality that is fundamental to one who is Self Realised, an understanding that all actions driven by strong emotions and feelings may lead to an unintended result which, on reflection later when passions have cooled, create regret and a search for forgiveness. Jesus understood that those doing this to Him were deluded and driven by the strong emotions and passions of the crowd. Such actions were not innate defining qualities of those mislead individuals who were behaving with such cruelty.

* * *

In Buddhism the Three Jewels are cornerstones of Buddhist belief and tell us to do no evil, to cultivate good and to purify our minds. In teaching the Middle Path the importance of moderation in achieving wisdom is underlined. Extremes in any form are to be avoided: of behaviour, ritual, eating and sleeping. Alongside this understanding the Buddhist Scripture *"Digha Nikaya"* speaks of the all-pervading power of love:

Put away all hindrances, let your mind full of love pervade one quarter of the world, and so too the second quarter, and so the third, and so the fourth. And thus the whole wide world, above, below, around and everywhere, altogether continue to pervade with love-filled thought, abounding, sublime, beyond measure, free from hatred and ill-will.

Buddhism in its Zen form provides a clear path to Self Realisation as we move towards seeing what it calls the "original face". The Rinzai Master, Daito Kokushi (1281–1337) gave this advice:

Every time a thought arises throw it away. Just devote yourself to sweeping away the thoughts. Sweeping away thoughts means performing zazen (sitting in meditation). *When thought is put down, the original face appears.*

This takes us straight into the Practice of Self Enquiry in two ways. Firstly before progress can be made towards Self Realisation the mind needs to be quietened and all thoughts set aside; secondly a question arises: just what is the nature of the original face and how will you know when you find it? The Practice in Self Enquiry seeks to achieve the first and find the answer to the second.

I will end this brief overview with a mention of the work of Sri Ramana Maharshi who reawakened interest in Self Enquiry in the early part of the 20th century. His teaching, and that of his disciple Sri HWL Poonja (Papaji), is grounded upon the ancient texts, notably *Bhagavad-Gita*, and I will leave you with this quotation from his key book *Be As You Are: The Teachings of Sri Ramana Maharshi*:

The Self... is as it is, ever-sparkling, ever steady, unmoving and unchanging. The individual confines himself to the limits of the changeful body or of the mind which derives its existence from the unchanging Self. All that is necessary is to give up this mistaken identity, and that done, the ever-shining Self will be seen to be the single non-dual reality.

* * *

Into the 1990s and the 21st century Self Enquiry, like many spiritual disciplines, has become Westernised, commercialised and enmeshed in verbiage turning the Practice into an intellectual exercise, ignoring the advice given by Sri Ramana when he suggested that we "... *leave off all this verbiage."*

Of greater concern, a cautionary tale should one be needed, is an understanding that many of the practitioners and teachers you will meet exploit the commercial potential of Self Enquiry, cashing in on the spiritual "naivety" of those who, no longer content with the material world, are searching for Truth. My advice is to tread with caution as you accept the invitations of a plethora of gurus and retreat facilitators established in centres across the globe, notably in India, offering you a path to Truth and probably at the same time inviting you to empty your pockets!

These books make for interesting, often challenging reading and will present you with views of the nature of True Self. However, the real answer, in Truth, is for you to find for yourself.

I would like to leave you with these words:

... if you're not always trying to be someone
You can be who you really are.
Tao Te Ching

Self Enquiry takes you directly to the place other paths eventually find.

3

The place of personal experience in Self Enquiry

You have within you all that is required to realise True Self. Close your eyes; be quiet for a while; focus your attention inwards to find the answer resting there.

What is the nature of True Self, the "I" that you are? Where does it reside and how can it be found? Can words be used to describe it or is it simply beyond description? As you study the texts, old and new, you will discover that many names have been used to "pin it down" followed by attempts to describe the nature of "I". By whatever name it is known – the Absolute, Atman, Spirit, Soul, Supreme Reality, Tathagata, Essence, Christ Consciousness, Original Face – the answers to these questions is not to be found in these books and spiritual texts no matter how wise and ancient they may be. They are the beliefs and opinions of others who have lived before you and walked their spiritual path. Nor is the answer to be found as you travel to faraway places and sit before the gurus, beautiful and inspiring as these experiences can be. The reading and the travelling may help in throwing a light across your path, presenting signposts for you to follow for a while or perhaps giving you useful tools to be placed in your self-help cupboard. This is their purpose.

It is your personal experience that holds the key and is the answer to these questions as you focus inwards applying the Practice to all that is presented to you as your life is lived in your body at this time on this Earth.

* * *

None of you can control what happens to you in life. Experiences are presented daily, by the minute; none of you can know "what is around the corner" even if you have convinced yourself that you know how to look and what to expect. Every experience carries a lesson which you may not recognise to be the case at the point of the experience; and yes it does seem to be a truism that the most painful and profound experiences have the most to teach you. It is unlikely, no matter how hard you might try, that any of you will avoid such experiences at some point in your life...

A few minutes before 7am on the morning of 2nd April 2001 I was plunged into a darkness the like of which I had never known before and for which nothing I had done previously prepared me. It was a darkness of such depth and breadth and seemingly endless, only slowly to lighten over time as all that I had to learn from the experience was learned. It was a darkness that overshadowed and undermined everything in life making even the most simple survival action seem pointless. Fourteen years on, these dark clouds can still sometimes gather as I reflect on this experience and continue to learn from it.

All of you at some point in life will feel grief, that most complex, powerful and many-layered emotion which will change and transform your view of life and its purpose, and carries with it the potential to undermine your life and health too. Although my beloved wife Kaisa had struggled with cancer for 18 years prior to her death and I had a sense that I would be "ready" and prepared for that time of letting go and acceptance, within seconds after her death I knew that this was not the case. I was not prepared in any way. I now confronted an experience of immense power and one with the potential to determine and colour every facet and dimension of the life that lay ahead.

From the beginning and throughout this experience, even on those darkest of days, there was an awareness somewhere from deep within me of a quiet voice becoming a little clearer and louder as time passed. Encouraged by this awareness I moved to a point, over time, when I was able to stand back and become a witness to my grief. I could feel an ineffable presence, something that remained untouched by this grief, gently supportive, leading me to understand that "I" was not defined by the grief I was experiencing nor by the loving relationship I was now having to relinquish. At times this unshakable presence felt like a "separate" identity to myself, untouched by this experience and living on, ever-present, a source of strength, hope and light.

Over time I came to recognise this Loving presence to be, in the words of Krishna in *Bhagavad-Gita*, *"The changeless spirit in the changeful flesh... "* untouched by all that is experienced. I have come to understand that the "I" that I am is not defined by the loving relationship I shared for over thirty-two years; nor is it defined by the grief I experienced when this ended although, at the time, it appeared to touch every part of me with such an overwhelming finality and the seeming power to bring my life to an end. Every part of me that is but my True Self, my Spirit, that which I Am...

You may have had an experience of similar intensity, often referred to as a moment of enlightenment, that becomes a benchmark in life, a point of measure for what has gone before and what may happen in the future. Many of you will not have such an experience or perhaps one awaits you at some other point in your life. There is no set rule, no determined way for setting you on the path. But you will know when you are there. Your experience in life, of **your** life not that of another, is at the heart of Self Enquiry, a deep well of learning for you to draw freely from as you need. This is the foundation for your Practice. It is the source of all you require in your personal search for Truth.

Thoughts arise, feelings come and go creating semblant realities, illusion all. The past exists only in your mind; the future that may be may not be also and is out of your control.

You too shall pass. In knowing this what is there to fear? Live life fully, lovingly, in total awareness.

Religions, beliefs, wise texts... As I understand it we move through these drawing from them what we need, grateful for the gift given, the light shown and the path revealed. Then we set them aside as our awareness blossoms of the ever-present presence of that which I Am.

4

The Practice: "Nan Yar: Who Am I?"

Trust is the key that opens the door that is itself an illusion.

The Practice outlined below is drawn from the Self Enquiry teachings. I have summarised it in this way to give you ease of access. Once learned it becomes a "meditation tool" with untold potential to be used anywhere, in any situation and with any thought, felt emotion or feeling. No special ritual or equipment is required, and practised daily you will come to use it instinctively without thought process as and when the need arises. It is to be used alongside the steps described in the following pages giving you plenty of "practice" for you to apply, with ease, in your everyday life. It is the key to what follows, a powerful tool with great potential to change your perception and understanding of you as you are, to quieten your mind and to bring you to that place of stillness and peace for which we all yearn yet so few of us appear to achieve.

The Practice
Go to a place where you will not be disturbed.
Be quiet for a moment.
With eyes closed observe your breathing.
When you are ready focus your attention inwards... Take your time...
There is no need to hurry...

Become the witness to your thoughts, feelings, anxieties, fears and doubts as they arise.
Go to the source: who is anxious, doubtful, fearful, who thinks that...?

I am, I do, me...

Then, when you are ready, ask the question:

"Who Am I?"

Remain with the question resisting the temptation to answer
through your mind.

Simply remain with the question, quietly, effortlessly...

"Who Am I?"

Follow this Practice with each thought as it arises. This will
probably mean in the early days you follow the procedure many
times! But stick with it and remain vigilant; and, yes, it may be
hard work to start with. The mind, desperate to maintain its
control over you, will ensure that it is! Thoughts come in many
guises: as doubt, anxiety, emotional turmoil or perhaps a
question. At the very point these arise proceed with the Practice.
Do not delay and do not be tempted to engage with the thought.
As the mind quietens, and it will over time, an awareness begins
to blossom as answers arise from within you, usually totally
unexpected in their timing and nature and from directions and
sources you would not think possible. But then you are no longer
thinking! You are stepping off this mind-driven merry-go-round
probably for the first time in your life. You are exploring new
territory which can be both scary and exciting as you step into
the unknown.

There is no time scale in what is essentially a process of reconditioning, of redefining, the nature of your relationship with
your mind. So, please, do not set yourself one; and remember too
that **learning and implementing this Practice on a regular basis,
at least once daily and probably more in the early days, is the
key to achieving success in the stages described in this book
and beyond**. The question itself, "Who Am I?", is simply a tool,
like the stick poking the fire that consumes untruth, false identification, fear, doubt and all the accumulated baggage of mind
and memory that has been your story, your identity, until this

moment. Ultimately the question itself is thrown on to the fire no longer required as True Self, that which you are, is realised.

The clouds have cleared, the garbage binned and the path now open for you to continue your journey.

Expecting nothing be ready for whatever arises...

Please note: this Practice, once learned, can be used in public places very effectively. At these times it may not be appropriate to close your eyes. If you are in a supermarket queue, a traffic jam etc. and you feel agitation arising begin by focusing on your breathing and then go into the Practice. Ask yourself: who is stressed, who is becoming anxious and frustrated? Next time you are in one of these places and feeling this way consider it an opportunity to apply the Practice and get into the habit of so doing. This is much better for you than becoming agitated and restless!

4. The Practice: "Nan Yar: Who Am I?"

There is nothing to fear, nothing to desire, nothing to know, nothing to believe.

Be who you are.

5

Step 1: I am not that...

You must relinquish all you have been to become who you are.

A perceived untrue self of false identification, born of mind driven by ego and social conditioning, controls your life determining how you live, behave, feel, think and exist.

Mind drives you to be that which you are not, convinces you that you are these things and then creates dependencies and habits which seem difficult, often impossible, to relinquish. Understanding this and breaking these chains is the first step of your journey in which you focus your attention on those layers of false identification, those things you are not, your story to this point and all the accumulated memories, the baggage which you are now invited to drop, to relinquish and to let go. In effect you are playing a "meditation game" in which you focus your attention on these layers of false identity, the crutches you lean on and the masks your mind has created. It will take considerable courage, you will feel resistance, anger perhaps, a fear of letting go, a nakedness and sense of exposure. The mind is desperate to remain in charge! But until this game has been played effectively, until all this baggage is dropped, your mind, the stronghold of resistance and suffering, will prevent you from proceeding further on your journey. You will remain in the fog immersed in darkness...

Go to a quiet place; focus on your breathing; look inwards and reflect:

The body I am in, the material things I possess, the job I do, the roles I play throughout my time in this body

27

_____I am not that;

The relationship I am in, my thoughts and memories, my desires and ambitions, the emotions I feel
_____I am not that.

The decisions I make, the things I have done in the past or that have been done to me and the actions I have taken
_____I am not that;

The religions I have followed, the teachings I have read, the beliefs and opinions I have held
_____I am not that.

These are semblant realities, objects of your perception, your individuality, your story to this point driving you to be that which you are not. It is your mind that determines this identity creating in you that burning desire to be "socially acceptable" or "good enough", perhaps more clever, beautiful, younger looking, more powerful or more spiritual. The picture is drawn and placed before you creating in your mind the image you are expected to realise. If you do not you will be considered a failure, you will not be accepted into the social fold, you will be an outcast. All of this is mind construct, of your mind and in your mind, ego-driven illusion, the product of your socialisation and conditioning to make you fit in, manipulable, compliant, to do as you are told and to believe all you are told without question.

Take your time and as much time as you need as you focus on each layer, gently moving through each area of identification as you confront and assess, without judgement, every aspect of your life to this point. Take one step at a time. There is no need to rush. It is very likely to be hard going with emotions and feelings arising then subsiding as you reflect on and question each area of your identity. It will seem like a roller-coaster ride and one you will quite often wish to get off! It is though essential that you see this part of the journey to its end.

With this stage of the work now confronted and complete, for many of us in the material-oriented and mind-driven West a most difficult and challenging stage, you are ready to travel on naked, yes, trembling, yes, perhaps somewhat fearful, yes, but less encumbered, with less baggage and free...

Free... !

Please go to the Practice.

Be quiet for a while and focus your attention inwards.

Your physical body, your possessions, your job, your relationships, your religion and beliefs, the decisions you make and actions you have taken in the past.

You are none of these things...

"Who Am I?"

You are addicted to thinking. A thought-seed, once planted, thrives on your attention, fear, imagination and expectations taking you on a roller-coaster journey into semblant reality leaving you wondering: where did it start? End this addiction in an instant. Be quiet for a moment, look inwards and ask: who thinks this, who believes this, who is tormented by this, who is being taken for a ride?

Me! I am!

Go to the source and ask:

"Who Am I?"

6

Step 2: Limitation is of the mind

Your mind is the source of your suffering. Only when controlled and quietened, through vigilant effort, will liberation be achieved and True Self realised.

Neither thought nor memory defines who you are.

In the Western world many of you are burdened with a mind that is, probably, the most dis-eased, garbage-filled and unbalanced on this Earth; a mind that is out of harmony with the natural world, with other human minds and with itself. Further, I suggest, for too long your mind has been used as a toilet by others with your permission to dump into it whatever they wish: beliefs, opinions, expectations, judgements, fear-induced behaviours and all degrees of indoctrination and misinformation. In turn, becoming fearful, ego-driven and desperate to please, the mind, in its desire to remain in control, places you on an ever-faster merry-go-round. You believe the lies and misinformation that fill it, becoming dizzy with all this pointless mind activity whilst becoming uncertain and distrustful of the nature of Truth and knowing where this rests.

The Westernised mind with its immeasurable store of memories and endless stream of thoughts has become the most powerful and dominating force in your life. Linked with its partner in control, the ego, it defines your day-to-day reality determining how you feel and behave. Throughout your life your mind creates seeming realities which you come to believe in and identify with as the defining "I". You believe totally and without question that the "I" you are is the "I" the mind tells you. You believe that you are the thoughts in your mind, turning subjectivity into objectivity, illusion into semblant reality. These thought-illusions, in becoming your identity, control you and determine how you live in every way: the opinions you hold, the fashions you follow, how you feel and behave, your diet, your emotional state and, over time, your physical health and well-being.

Yet your mind, in being a complex collection of memories and thoughts, is itself nothing more than an illusion deceiving you into believing it exists; and you believe it absolutely. Few of you have ever considered questioning its existence since for so long it has appeared to be an integral part of who you **think** you are. But I invite you to reflect for a moment and take a step back from this machinating and restless mind. Become a witness to its ceaseless activity. Observe how it works somewhere within your brain and ask yourself: what is the mind? Does it exist like the brain? Would it appear on an X-Ray image? Can it be physically handled, removed from the body and presented in a physical form for dissection and analysis?

No it cannot be. Mind has no physical form. Every aspect of your life is controlled by something that does not exist! This is a revelation of a high order is it not? So I will say it again. The mind is an illusion. You are controlled by something that does not exist!

Whilst you reflect on this revelation consider another question. Can the mind be quietened by the mind? This in itself is a thought, and a desire to find an answer will keep your mind busy in its efforts to justify its existence. It will drive you to seek answers "out there": in different meditation techniques, yoga, exotic rituals, chanting, breath control, perhaps convince you to change how you dress or your diet and even your name. Once again you will be placed on a merry-go-round becoming the doer of things that you hope will bring you relief and some peace. Sadly, though, the sedative effect of these activities, like tranquilisers or alcohol, is short-lived and soon fades returning you to where you began. Thoughts arise again and with them more anxiety, fear and ego-driven behaviour.

No the mind cannot be quietened by the mind. It is like trying to wash away a flood with a bucket of water! Only when the rain stops will the flood drain away. Similarly the mind will only quieten as the Practice in Self Enquiry is applied, with vigilance, to each thought as it arises.

If there were no thoughts and memories there would be no mind. Both mind and ego do not exist. In Self Enquiry, as the Practice is employed, the mind quietens, memories of past experiences lose their grip on you and the ego vanishes. You begin to drop the baggage carried for so long in your life, the false identities fall away. As the fog lifts and the clouds disperse you see more clearly the path upon which you are walking.

You have now "*... shaken off those tangled oracles which ignorantly guide...* " (*Bhagavad-Gita*). Unencumbered, with lighter step you are free to continue your journey.

6. Step 2: Limitation is of the mind

A thought can determine how you feel but it does not define who you are.

The ephemeral thought process begins and ends; you are eternal.

Our second step into the Practice focuses on this observation: that limitation is of the mind.

The merry-go-round mind, always happy to take you for a ride, creates semblant realities and identities which you believe totally and without question define who you are. Masks are created for you to hide behind, crutches for you to lean on and habits become dependencies which, in having the power to control you, are difficult to relinquish. Your mind fills with thoughts and accumulates memories becoming ever-heavier baggage carried throughout your life; your story to this point seeming to be that which you are. The only place these things exist is in your mind. They are in the mind and of the mind. They are the clouds blocking the sun:

I cannot do this_____

I am not creative_____

I am a failure_____

I am too fat or too thin_____

I am not good enough_____

I believe this to be true_____

This is right_____

This is wrong_____

These are self-limiting thoughts. In whom do they arise? What is their source? Whenever a thought arises stop it in its tracks by becoming a witness to it, refraining from giving it your attention as you ask, "Who is thinking this?" and answer "I am"... In then asking "Who Am I?" you will take the "I" thought back to its source... The merry-go-round will slowly cease to turn.

Please return to the Practice. Be quiet for a while and focus inwards. I am not my thoughts nor am I the story of my past.

"Who Am I?"

6. Step 2: Limitation is of the mind

The walls built around you are an illusion; the prison gates do not exist. The machinations of mind, once quietened and relinquished, leave you free to be who you are.

Limitation is of the mind.

7

Step 3: Unlearning the learned

The time will come when you will set aside all you have learned and all effort ends. With blossoming awareness you will come to see that you are your master, your guru and your guide.

As you prepare to take the next step of your journey you are becoming aware that you are developing a different kind of relationship with your mind. In clearing the baggage held there for so long and with the lifting of the fog, your mind is ceasing to be the controller and enslaver. Its hold over you is easing. As the mind quietens it is learning to be of service to you whilst you recognise it to be a useful tool in everyday life. Now you are ready to take the next step: to empty the mind still further as you set aside all you have learned.

Since your childhood you have undergone a process of conditioning when your mind has been filled with a multitude of things others consider worthy of learning. In your desire to please them you have studied hard, read many books and absorbed many facts and a great deal of knowledge. The things you have learned appear to define how you see yourself and who you think you are. The effort you make to learn more becomes the purpose of your existence, of life itself. You strive endlessly to realise the picture of expectation drawn for you by your parents or teachers often to a point of anxiety and perhaps despair when it becomes clear to you that you cannot fulfil this. Theories, beliefs and opinions, usually gathered from books or whilst listening to those deemed wiser than you, are internalised to the point of believing to be your own.

* * *

Alongside this mental activity that other powerful force, social conditioning beginning at birth, drives you to become this or that tempting you with material gain, status and power if you "do well". As your life progresses in this body you are smothered with many role-playing layers, beginning in childhood; striving to "do well" or maybe failing at school; perhaps becoming a student at college. Moving on to young adulthood you become a partner, husband or wife, mother or father carrying many different lesser roles: counsellor, scapegoat, banker, taxi driver etc. In work, or unemployed, perhaps disabled and unable to work, maybe loaded with financial success... On and on it goes, endless possibilities, roles and labels as you move into middle and old age. Each layer placed upon you, each label attached to you, carries with it conformity to a set of behavioural patterns and rules which you are unwise to ignore. Layer upon layer covers you until any awareness of True Self, who you are, appears to be lost, smothered and choked to near-death.

For your mind and ego these are times of feasting! The endless effort you make to conform, to "prove" yourself, to be worthy becomes the be all and end all of your very existence. It becomes your identity, who you think you are or crave to be, how you see yourself and how you want others to see you.

Later in life you begin to feel a sense of dissatisfaction, a restlessness, an awareness that no matter how much of this learning you do, this material stuff you accumulate around you or how senior and well-paid your position in work, something appears to be missing. Acquiring any number of new cars or obtaining an even more lucrative job is simply no longer fulfilling for you, leaving a feeling of emptiness within you. You become aware of a need for "self-development" although remain unsure of what this really means. You begin to sense that there is something worthwhile and fulfilling to be found beneath and beyond all these imposed layers. You now embark on that elusive search for "enlightenment" about which you have heard so much. Your search to discover what this is drives you to study more books and wise spiritual texts, perhaps change your diet and how you dress, attend courses and retreats, travel to faraway places and absorb more beliefs and opinions. Wide-eyed, like a moth to the flame you are drawn to the guru's honeyed voice and texts of wisdom believing the answer is to be found there. The merry-go-round continues to turn.

It would be wrong of me to suggest to you that this wealth of knowledge is useless. It can in fact be used and applied in many different ways just as a toolbox has a collection of tools which can be put to many purposes. If somebody asks me to show them how to paint I will not just throw them a paintbrush and paints and tell them to get on with it. There are skills to teach, facts to learn about different papers and paints and then, when the student is ready, I will direct them towards exploring the materials, to tap into their heart-centred creativity and see what happens.

As life is lived you will be drawn to different texts, different teachers, and different sets of opinion. Study them as and when you need and then set them aside when you have learned from them what you require. You will know when the time has come to do this, to relinquish this effort, to set aside these once-useful tools which have now served their purpose for you.

Learn to look beyond the written page, the wise script, the soft voice of the guru and the flickering screen. Learn to learn from your direct experience, and as you learn from this experience focus your attention inwards. An awareness grows that much of what you have learned needs to be unlearned. The rest needs to be set aside, its task for you completed. The mind-mass of others' opinions, belief systems and dogma, much of it baggage in itself, is a rich manure maintaining the life of mind and keeping you firmly attached to a false sense of Self. It is time to set it all aside.

With blossoming awareness you will come to know that you

are your teacher and your guide. You have within you all you require to realise True Self, to be who you are.

Please go to the Practice.

Be quiet, focus on your breathing and look inwards.

All you have learned, all the expectations placed upon you, the demands made of you and the roles you have played.

You are none of these things.

"Who Am I?"

7. Step 3: Unlearning the learned

Seasons change, bodies change and die, minds change and relationships end.

But Love felt in Truth, that which you are, endures.

8

Step 4: Relinquish Desire

Sometimes it feels as if you are destroying yourself and yet True Self, that which you are, cannot be touched. It is the shackles that are being broken, the garbage offloaded, and your story to this point that is falling away as mind quietens, ego vanishes and all desires end.

Desire, born of mind and fuelled by ego, can exert a strong hold over you. Desire grows from your attachment to the physical world of the body and the material world of ownership and possession: you must look like this, behave like this, have this well-paid job, be this successful person, own the latest mobile phone or fast car and so on and so forth. Desire is suffused with expectation and ambition centring around personal gain and profit or seeking to be "better" than someone else. Desire exerts considerable influence over your ability or inability to realise True Self; it is a chain holding you back from being who you are, a dark cloud blocking the sun.

Desire gives birth to strong emotions and feelings and a craving for social status, money, power and sexual gratification. The strength of a desire can lead you to behave in a way that is contrary to your nature. You need this, you want that, you must have whatever it is your heart is set upon at any cost driving you to be that which you are not. Often, an unintended consequence, you are taken to a place of personal despair, anger and suffering when you are denied that which you so desperately seek or wish to keep. Relationships break down, a loved one dies, a well-paid job ends and the body ages and eventually dies. In relinquishing your dependency on and desire for these things, for many of you a painful and challenging process in itself, you are free to travel on, to take the next step on your path to Self Realisation.

All desire is limitation, even the desire to be free of desire. Stand back, be quiet for a moment; become a witness to your desires and see them for what they are: distractions and sideshows to that which matters placing you, once again, on a mind and ego-driven merry-go-round difficult to step off.

Look within. Go to the Source. You are not that which you desire.

Desire to know but one thing, who you are.

"Who Am I?"

8. Step 4: Relinquish Desire

It matters not what I, you or they think or believe.
Something is what it is and will be what is determined.
The wisdom comes in accepting this.

9

Step 5: Feeling and Emotion

It takes but a single flame to dispel the darkness.

The journey through Life is one of many side roads and distractions, leafy lanes and pathways and, sometimes, rocky places where you would perhaps rather not be. You never know how you will feel the next day, the next hour or moment and what will be placed before you. You may feel happy one moment then the next, for no clear reason, depressed and anxious. Perhaps you have been upset by something you have seen on the TV or been told by a friend. Perhaps from somewhere deep within you a memory has arisen, triggered by a simple event or experience – a fragrance, a piece of music, an image, an old photograph – turning on an emotional tap that totally changes your present state. Emotions arise from within you determining how you feel and behave; they can exert a strong hold over you influencing your actions and reactions in that moment. Then, like the dark clouds crossing the sun, they are gone.

Some are strong emotions deeply felt, never more so than at this time of upheaval and change. The death of one you love; the ending of a relationship with one you still love; the endless exploitation and destruction of our beautiful Mother Earth; the needless and pointless brutality of war, social injustice and poverty... These are the emotional sledgehammers experienced in life that seem set to knock you off course, succeeding perhaps for a while, making you question the point and value of your existence and even whether you still wish to be a part of it.

Then anger becomes rage as you stand by helpless, perhaps desperate to know what to do and how to help ease your pain and that of another. Jealousy becomes resentment felt at the

1

achievements of others. The burning craving for power and wealth drives you to behave in ways contrary to your nature. The despair felt by so many of you at the natural ageing process of the body, accompanied by a growing awareness of your own mortality, may, in turn, drive you to find ways, often extreme, to conceal the fact that you will grow old. These are strong emotions which give rise to stronger feelings that appear to have such a grip on you with the power to determine your physical and mental well-being.

* * *

Then there is joy, bliss and happiness, the emotions you feel at the birth of a child, securing your new job, marrying one you love, walking into nature or winning the lottery. These beautiful and exciting experiences create in you feelings and emotions that you want to last forever and yet seem so easily dashed by the dark clouds that gather.

Experience these emotions fully. Do not suppress them or pretend they are not being felt in that moment. Then express them fully in whatever way works for you: shout, scream, cry, laugh, dance, protest and join Greenpeace or paint a picture. Then, when all is expressed and peace returns to you, end all attachment to the experience and set it aside grateful for the lesson learnt.

Whatever you think and feel and however you are driven to behave rest assured the tide will ebb and flow, the trees will leaf and blossom in the spring and the sun will shine. It is the machinations of mind, emotion and feeling which present you with these seeming realities driving you to be that which you are not.

Stand back from this turmoil and torment; become the witness to these emotions and feelings as they arise from within you. They are but sideshows and distractions to that which matters, impermanent, ever-changing and soon to pass. They do not define who you are.

Close your eyes, take a few deep breaths. Focus on the Practice, quietly, and ask:

"Who feels this, who is angry, who is upset?
I do, I am, me... "

"Who Am I?"

The mind with all its attachments is the root of your suffering, clouding Self Realisation.

On being free of thought-illusion you are free to be who you are, then, now, always.

10

Step 6: Conscience, action and behaviour

End this illusion by ceasing to believe in it.

The word "conscience" of itself creates concern and anxiety within you, appearing to have its own momentum and energy in taking you on the "guilt trip" so many speak of experiencing, usually for no clear reason and little purpose; and how easily this is stirred! I have worked with people from all walks of life who have deeply enjoyed the creative work we have done together. On being asked, "Did you enjoy this?" I remember one participant answered, "Yes, very much indeed, but I feel guilty!" "Feeling guilty for what reason?" I asked. "Because I have enjoyed myself! I should really be at home doing the housework..." I was really quite surprised by this comment at the time but wonder: how many of you have felt this way?

The word "conscience" does carry a particular meaning for most of us, hammered into us as children during the process of growing up, the social conditioning most of us experienced when we were trained to fit in, to conform, to follow the rules determined by our sex, social class, religion and politics. A picture may well have been drawn for you and placed before you clearly outlining what you are expected to become at home, at school, in your work, in relationships, in parenthood and all those other layers of social manipulation. Should you "fail" to meet these expectations you are punished in some way by being excluded, reprimanded, criticized or judged, reinforcing in you a sense of not being "good enough". Lasting damage is done impacting on and colouring future behaviour and actions which, if judged by others to be inadequate or "wrong", result in a "guilty conscience" arising from within you which in itself leads to suffering and is hard to relinquish. It seems an endless cycle difficult to break, a fear-driven merry-go-round difficult to step off. Its control and stranglehold over you appears to be unbreakable.

Conscience then could be described as the not-so-silent policeman planted firmly in your mind by parents, teachers and other well-meaning adults, the spokespersons of the society into which you are born. It grows into a force which controls all your actions and behaviour throughout your life. It becomes a chain which represses you and the walls that imprison you, holding you back from being who you are. In essence it is once again a construct of the mind, the only place it exists, illusion all yet seeming so real, making it the hardest to set aside because it is so deeply ingrained.

However, in Self Enquiry there is a different understanding of this powerful force we in the West call conscience, described in *Bhagavad-Gita* as *"a Master in the Hearts of men"*. It is regarded as an integral part of True Self, of that which you are. Conscience is a quiet awareness, a voiceless voice which guides your actions whilst gently pointing the way. It is beyond your control so therefore any effort made to control it is a waste of your energy. Conscience guides you, effortlessly, quietly, to act in ways that reflect your true nature, that which you are. Heart-centred and directed it can do no wrong. It is a guiding voice that is ignored at your peril, something often experienced when you follow the usually louder voice of your mind and ego instead.

As life is lived emotion and feeling give rise to action and action gives rise to emotion and feeling. At some later stage in your life, perhaps many years after the event that caused you to feel and behave as you did, when your emotions have quietened and your perceptions changed, you may experience a sense of regret at an action taken at that time, giving rise to this so-called "guilty conscience". From a perspective of calm and reason, perhaps some years on and with a "more mature" understanding of things, you realise you reacted or behaved in a way contrary to your nature, the consequence of emotional upheaval and turmoil felt at that moment, something over which you had no control. How often do you regret something you did in the past, realise you behaved badly, know you would do better given a second chance or wish you could simply turn back the clock and start again? This regret is often spoken of in Satsang relating to experiences and actions taken in the past, many in distant childhood, but still being carried by the mind many years on, festering away unresolved and at the root of suffering.

With this understanding, this blossoming awareness, you come to realise that you are not defined by your actions or behaviour at any time in your life when you were driven by strong emotions and feelings over which you had no control. Perhaps you were angry, grief-stricken, desperate and in deep pain resulting in your losing control of your physical responses and hitting out or saying something hurtful, often to one you love. In turn someone you know and love may have been experiencing similar emotional turmoil and upheaval at a time when you were nearby and they struck out at you hurting you in some way, verbally, perhaps even physically. Understanding this removes any need for judgement of yourself and your actions and behaviour and those of another towards you.

* * *

As you continue on your journey applying this Practice to all that arises from within you, mind and ego will quieten and subside and with this the urge to do all mind and ego driven activity. As you travel on more layers are being removed, more baggage dropped and more chains broken. An awareness grows stronger of that voiceless voice, that quiet, heart-centred guide at the root of all behaviour, an ineffable presence in need of no words to describe it. In this re-defined form conscience is recognised to be an integral part of True Self, that which you are. It is a quiet awareness guiding your actions. Ego-free, fear-free, desireless, aware yet unattached to the outcome of any action and coming from a place of love and compassion you will do no wrong. Instinctively you behave in a way that will not inflict suffering, your conscience stirring you to act in accordance with your true nature, one of Heart-felt Love.

The "guilty conscience", along with all the other mind-created baggage, is consigned to the past. It no longer exists. You are free.

Please return to the Practice.

Whenever a sense of guilt arises from within you or as a consequence of the words or behaviour of another step back a little. Focus on your breathing and ask:

"Who feels this way? Who is judging, who feels the guilt? I do, I am, me…"

"Who Am I?"

Be vigilant lest the pointing finger blocks the moon, the mirror becomes the icon.

Once the message is understood set the messenger aside like a map of the journey now known.

11

Step 7: Be in your body but not of it

End your attachment to and dependency on all that is perishable. Death is the shedding of an old overcoat, age but the ageing of physical body.

How can there be an end to that which has no beginning?

You came into your body with nothing. You had no name, no mind, no ego and no personality. You also owned nothing and therefore had no attachment or addiction to any material thing. When your journey is complete in this life your body, like an old overcoat now well worn, will be set aside as you leave it, empty-handed so to speak, taking nothing with you.

At the root of suffering is your attachment to your body and the degree to which you identify with it as being you, defining who you are. You are deeply fearful that its death will be the end of you. Therefore, to protect yourself from this awareness of your physical mortality, you take all sorts of measures to prop up a false sense of security which, you hope, will shield you from the inevitable ageing process. Your well-paid job, your possessions and accumulated wealth, the relationships you are in and, of course, all the measures you take to keep your body looking young become the crutches you lean on and the masks you hide behind. Endless effort is made to assist you in denying the natural ageing process which will, yes, lead to the inevitable death of the body. At no time in history has there been such paranoia and fear surrounding the thought of ageing and death driving so many in the Western world, of all ages, to resort to desperate and often extreme measures designed to slow the ageing process of the physical body, or at least stop it showing.

All to no avail of course as you remain imprisoned by your paranoia knowing you cannot prevent the inevitable.

Your next step on your journey is to surrender this attachment to all that is perishable, to accept that no matter how much you want to hold on to something, own something, love something or desire something it will eventually be lost to you. Nothing is permanent. In surrendering this attachment you are free from your dependency on all of these things: body, possessions and relationships. You can remove the masks and kick away the crutches to enjoy a freedom and lightness that you have never felt before and whilst you are still alive! You are in your body for a short while to experience fully, to learn fully, and to celebrate life fully on your journey into Truth.

* * *

So how should you care for your body? Advice is on hand in the teachings. Siddhartha Gautama (Buddha) for example, after years of austerity and deprivation during which he came close to death, realised that a healthy body was necessary if one were to be successful in the pursuit of wisdom. If you destroy your body before reaching journey's end what has been the point? He taught of the importance of following the Middle Path which lies between extreme deprivation and ritual and excessive eating and sleeping, acknowledging the close relationship of a healthy body with Self Realisation. *Bhagavad-Gita* is also clear in its advice recommending moderation in eating, exercise and taking rest in that place of "... *true piety which most removes Earth-aches and ills...*" Sri Ramana Maharshi in his teaching suggests the eating of *sattvic* (pure) food in moderation will increase that quality within the mind.

Extreme behaviour, therefore, in any form is bad for you! In a healthy approach to physical, mental and spiritual well-being there is no place for excess or extremes. You are advised to avoid excessive eating and physical exercise, extreme vigil, ritual and the deprivation of rest and sleep. Such extremes are detrimental to successful meditation and physical well-being and have no place in Self Enquiry. Balance and moderation is advised in all these activities. You are invited to take good care of your body. Eat wholesome, organic food prepared with love; take gentle exercise regularly and rest too. Walk into nature as often as you can. Express your body fully in every way as you sing, dance, make cakes and enjoy your sexuality. Celebrate being alive totally and in every way knowing when the time comes your body will die. In no attachment to or dependency on all that is perishable there is liberation, freedom. Remember:

Be in your body but not of it.

Now please return to the Practice. Whilst you will look after your body and enjoy all that it brings you are not defined by your physical presence.

Be quiet for a moment, focus your attention inwards.
You are not your body.

"Who Am I?"

11. Step 7: Be in your body but not of it

All actions will be taken in complete awareness of the outcome and with no desire for reward.

Every loving act, no matter how small it may seem, brings peace to you and all around you.

Love Eternal: This I Am.

12

Step 8: Earth Matters

Said simply: if the Earth that sustains us is so undermined that she can no longer support all that lives human endeavour, no matter how noble, will be rendered useless.

In destroying the Earth you also are destroyed.

The wise continue to tell us that all is well in this moment; and yet there is this underlying dis-comfort and unease, this painful awareness, that this is not so. All is not well. We live in a time when humankind, notably those with a Western ego-driven mind, has never been more disconnected from Mother Earth and the energy and power of natural forces and change. Many of us are totally insensitive towards and uncaring of the very planet that sustains and nurtures us. We continue to fail to make this vital connection: in destroying the Earth we are destroying ourselves, nothing less. There is so much pain and disease, so much suffering, so much war in communities and lands across the globe, something of which we are more aware than ever before thanks to easy access to modern communications. Ignorance can no longer be an excuse for lack of concern and action yet many of us, it seems, simply do not care as politicians and corporate businesses across the globe undermine those who do.

The killing of our precious Mother Earth continues at an unprecedented rate alongside an increasing awareness amongst us that this is so. Yet many of us stand idly by continuing to consume, as if by right, the Earth's resources whilst giving nothing back. In the name of greed, profit and so-called progress the Earth is being sacrificed, raped and polluted to the point of extinction at all levels. The inevitable impact upon the natural world of this relentless exploitation is being denied or censored by those who, fully understanding the consequences and purpose of their actions, are hoping that those who care and are prepared to make a stand will just go away in despair or simply give up.

* * *

Earth matters. The Earth is essential to the very existence and well-being of all living creatures, something humankind has known and honoured since the beginning of time and totally ignored as Western culture has taken root. The warnings have been issued by the ancient tribes and, increasingly in this time of climate change, by the Earth herself. All are ignored or dismissed by those in power or big business who describe these warnings as alarmist, untrue, detrimental to progress and, more often than not, damaging to the profits being made from the continued exploitation of Earth's natural resources to fuel an ever-greedy and unsustainable lifestyle.

But these warnings are ignored at our peril. Long overdue now is the understanding and acknowledgement of the connection between personal health and well-being and the plight of the Earth. Examples abound. Just one of many is the alarming increase in serious illnesses like cancer and multiple sclerosis linked to the poisons we pump into the environment which have a detrimental effect on all levels of the food chain whilst undermining the quality of soil, air and water, the very essence of life. The wealth of evidence verifying this can no longer be ignored or dismissed.

It is important to bring this discussion directly into our own lives. Ask yourself: "What am I doing to contribute to the Earth's plight; and what can I do to change things?" A great deal on both counts as it happens, whether you know it or not. Many of us rarely acknowledge that with every action there is an outcome. Or if we do and it is controversial or upsetting in any way we repress what we have discovered or deny it ever happened. Many of us find it hard to accept that a personal action can be responsible for anything. It is always somebody else who is at fault, somebody else who should clear up the mess. Every action taken by every individual, positive or negative, no matter how insignificant it feels, will make a difference. Living with awareness and acknowledging this responsibility as guests living upon this Earth is an important step in your journey towards Truth.

"Contaminate your bed and you will one night suffocate in your own waste." (Chief Seattle, 1854) That night is now upon us, everywhere and in every land, casting its dark shadow across the lives of many generations to come.

* * *

What of spirituality in this conversation? In the often rarefied and esoteric world of spiritual study and devotion earthly matters are regarded as unimportant and of little concern. Considered intrusive and tedious such issues are a distraction to spiritual awakening. For many declaring themselves to be on a spiritual path an invitation to focus inwards is taken as an invitation to turn away from the outside world. Little concern is shown for the health of the planet whilst earthly matters are considered a distraction to spiritual practice.

But does spiritual practice demand as a condition that you must withdraw from earthly concerns and retreat from the world? In Self Enquiry a clear "no" is given to this question. As you pursue your spiritual practice you are to remain firmly connected to the world in which you live and work, remaining aware of and acting on the responsibilities you carry.

Humanity did not create this Earth and is not responsible for it. The Earth can look after herself and will do so long after the extinction of humanity. However, with the growing awareness that Self Enquiry brings into your life you come to understand that the way you live will impact in some way on the Earth. As a custodian of the Earth, living in awareness, you will ensure that any action you take will not harm the Earth or any living creature. Every action taken by every individual will make a difference no matter how small it may seem.

In Self Enquiry then clear direction is given. As you pursue your spiritual practice your feet remain firmly on the ground respecting the Earth that sustains you. You will remain connected to your everyday life, at work and at home, actively engaged with all that arises whilst inwardly remaining calm, unaffected and still. You are aware that every action you take has an outcome; you live honourably doing no harm to all that lives. You live lovingly taking from the Earth that which is needed, with thanks, and giving back to the Earth that which she needs. Such loving action, heartfelt, brings peace into your life and to everything around you.

Living today on a planet that seems itself to be struggling for survival there is wisdom in learning a Practice that equips you to process the potentially destructive emotions that arise from within you: fear, anxiety, anger, helplessness and despair. Self Enquiry does this becoming a means to personal "survival" and acceptance, and one which equips you to move forward with love and strength, empowered to make your contribution to the essential changes humankind must make in its relationship with Mother Earth and all sentient beings.

* * *

God is often asked by those in despair how He could permit so much violence and suffering on the Earth He created. In asking this question, I wonder, is humanity relinquishing the part it has played in creating the seedbed for this violence and destruction? Rather than continuing to blame God for the catastrophes now befalling humanity I humbly suggest that it is time we all accepted fully our role as custodians and protectors of this Earth and all that live upon her and act accordingly.

What we do unto this Earth we do unto ourselves.

In your Practice begin by focusing on this thought:

Ask no longer what this Earth can do for you; ask instead what you can do for this Earth.

Be still for a moment; close your eyes and take a deep breath. Focus your attention inwards:

"Who Am I?"

As life is experienced and shared with all that lives on this precious Earth each action I take will be in awareness of its potential outcome.
Unique as I am there is no separation and so much shared feeling, common ground upon which to stand for me to support you and you me.

When the time comes for me to surrender earthly matters I will do so with love leaving behind an Earth enriched by my presence.

13

Step 9: On Unity

Be Buddhist, there is duality; be Hindu there is duality; be Christian there is duality; be atheist there is duality. Be your True Self there is non-duality, unity with God and all that lives on our precious Mother Earth.

Your suffering arises as a consequence of your attachment to the physical body, from the endless energy expended in meeting the infinite and ever-changing demands of mind and ego that operate within it and from your perception of your isolation in seeing yourself as an individual moving within an objective, often hostile world. The world out there, even beyond your own front door, is often perceived as threatening, unwelcoming, a place to roam with caution filled as it is with different religions, belief systems, social classes and hierarchies in which you do not feel safe or welcome. Your perceived individuality, your separation and isolation, is a product of your Westernised mind. Once again it is an illusion but one that seems so real to you. The only place it exists is in your mind.

Taken further consider your relationship with all Sentient Beings and the Earth herself: the animals and plants, the sky, the soil, the sea. When did you last focus on the beauty of a flower, listen to birdsong, get your hands muddy, or experience that deep peace as you walked by the sea or in a wood? Separation, alienation, them and us: this is normality in the Western world in which all this beauty, this life, is either ignored or there to be exploited and put to profitable use rather than embraced with love as kindred living spirit.

Taken further still, consider for a moment the nature of your relationship with God. What is that like? In the predominantly

Christian West you have been conditioned to believe that God exists somewhere out there, outside yourself. Deeply embedded into your mind is a picture of Him sitting resplendent in His Heaven somewhere beyond the sky looking down upon you usually with benevolence surveying all He has created. He is there for you to worship, to pray to when you need help and spiritual guidance, and to seek forgiveness for your sins. He is the power and force behind all creation, separate from you and on a different level entirely. If you are "good" in this life your sins will be forgiven. You will meet Him after your death and live peacefully forever in His heaven.

* * *

It probably goes without saying, however, that one of the greatest causes of division and separation in humanity is religious dogma and the different belief systems that have grown from it. Throughout history Christian is set against Muslim, non-Christian against Christian, Protestant against Catholic and so on, contrary it must be said to the teaching of those at the forefront of these religions: Jesus Christ, Allah, Buddha and Krishna. The countless wars fought throughout history in the name of religion are contrary to the teachings those who are in conflict claim to represent.

Self Enquiry embraces Advaita, non-duality, unity, a single non-dual reality. There is no separation, no division between True Self, God and all that lives upon this planet. God is in you and you are in God; as you contemplate the beauty of a single flower you are looking into the eyes of God. Living in a place of stillness, love-filled, there is no conflict. All are One. In being True Self, who you are, there is unity with God, with fellow human beings and with all that live on this precious Earth; and love, felt in Truth, is at the heart of everything.

God, Brahman, Atman, Supreme Reality, Allah, Buddha, True

Self... by whatever name all are This: Love, peace and unity. I will close this stage of your journey with these beautiful words:

"I am He whom I Love and He whom I Love is I."
Mansur Hallaj

Please return to the Practice. Be still for a while.
Focus inwards. Unique as you are there is no separation...

"Who Am I?"

It is said and often believed that my thoughts have made me who I am. But how can this be?

The ephemeral thought process begins and ends.
The I that I Am is eternal.

Step 10: Be free

Freedom is your birthright, love defines who you are. Your mind, creating semblant realities, illusion all, is for you to tame until quietness reigns supreme, liberation is achieved and your True Self realised.

Many of you are living a lie as you engage with a multitude of mind games, never-ending it seems, driven by ego and that most deeply-held desire to "fit in", to be "good enough" and to be socially acceptable. Over time the accumulated garbage produced along the way obliterates any sense of True Self, who you are, your sense of direction and purpose lost as you struggle to achieve some sense of peace. This anguish is at the root of your suffering as you seek to meet the endless demands of mind and ego. You are enslaved as the ceaseless doer, achiever and changer of things seeing yourself as individual, separate, moving within an objective and often unloving world.

Just reflect for a moment on your past behaviour and the forces that have driven it. Become the witness to your life story, your history, avoiding the temptation to make judgements. You did this, believed that, travelled here, wore this and listened to that ever-fearful of "failing", perhaps concerned that you will be judged by others as "unworthy". Like a dog chasing its tail, endlessly, until you are dizzy, you return to where you began: the doer doing, the fixer fixing, the seeker seeking. The mind follows whilst the ego feasts leaving you wondering what has been achieved. This is "normality" for you, your everyday existence, tiring, exhausting and, yes, largely pointless.

But understand this, another revelation: you are imprisoned in a place that is only "real" in your mind. The walls built around you are mind-created illusion; the prison gates do not exist. All you need to do to dispel this illusion is cease to believe in it! Break just a single link in the chain that holds you back and it will fall from you, forever.

As your mind quietens the prison walls crumble, the gates open and the chains fall away. Freedom blossoms of itself as you step off the crazy mind-driven merry-go-round, kick away the crutches and remove the masks that for so long have alienated you from who you are. This is the purpose of this journey, of the Practice, of Self Enquiry: to reunite you with True Self, who you are, that which is always present within you.

* * *

You understand now that you have no control over any experience placed before you. Your task is to learn from that experience, to experience the experience fully then, when that is done, to set this aside too. Whatever is determined to happen will happen, whatever is not will not. You now know that no amount of effort, worry or anxiety will change things so you can relax, stand back, become a witness to events as they happen, your reactions to these events and the emotions arising from within you. Then, after reflection from a place of peace, you will act accordingly, resolve the issue and move on. You are free from the mind-driven demands and expectations that have for so long created fear, anxiety and dependency in you appearing to define who you are.

The mind can only entertain one thought at a time so think this:

I am free!

As other thoughts seek to undermine this, to take control, to replace the chains, think again:

I am free!

Your freedom comes in freeing yourself from identification with mind-body-ego and all the associated baggage. Now free of desire, expectation, fear, and anxiety you experience a sense of liberation and peace the like of which you have never known before...

Please return to the Practice.

Go to the Source, be re-united with your True Self. You are free, unburdened, uncluttered, unchained.

Free to be who you are.

"Who Am I?"

The 'isms are explored, the wise books read, the sacred places
visited, the honeyed voice of the guru has filled your ears.
Now take rest, be quiet and focus inwards as you ask "Who
Am I?"

Why circumvent the globe when you are already home?

15

Step 11: I Am This...

True Self is beyond mind and imagination and requires no words. True Self is what it is: Source, Absolute, unbounded, complete, pure and perfect Consciousness.

Love Eternal: I Am This.

In silence with eyes closed you have focused your attention inwards, effortlessly. The Practice is now a way of life used instinctively without thought process, available for you wherever you are and with whatever you are confronted. As your mind sinks into stillness an awareness blossoms of a quiet, voiceless presence, ever-present. The question "Who Am I?" as the stick poking the fire has consumed untruth, fear, false identification, doubt and all the accumulated baggage of mind and memory that has been your story, your identity, to this point.

Soon the question itself is thrown on to the fire no longer required. Like the drops of rain merging with the ocean all thoughts have returned to Source. True Self, that which you are, is realised. You are no longer what others have told you to be or society demands of you. You are who you are. This shining Truth, who you are, is for you to find as you focus your attention inwards. Trusting that this is so as you set aside all mind-generated resistance is the key unlocking the door that is itself an illusion.

As you move further on your journey the silences become longer and deeper, the need for words lessens and you move with increasing ease and lightness. The baggage has been thrown out the window, the layers of false identification have been removed; the chains are broken and you no longer need to hide behind the masks. Your mind is now quietened and with it the ego and all the associated behaviour has vanished. The page has turned, the last train gone; there is no going back even if this is desired or possible. As the fog lifts and the clouds clear you are reunited with your True Self. You are at peace with your Self and everything around you. You are home.

* * *

From time to time the clouds will gather and the fog will descend blocking the sun. Desires, long-held mental habits and deep-felt emotions will continue to challenge you. Doubt may arise. But remember to stand back from all this, become a witness to this feeling also and ask: Who is doubtful? What is there to doubt? You have been on a remarkable journey of transformation and change embracing a process of reconditioning every aspect of your being. You have worked to rid yourself of long-held beliefs, desires, deeply felt emotions, ego-driven activity and old mental habits, the very fabric of the life you have known up to this time, your identity, who you believed you were. Your resolve will continue to be tested as new thoughts arise and new experiences are placed before you. Do not to engage with these, do not attach any importance to them, avoid giving them any power or hold over you; learn from the experiences that which you need and set them aside too. The clouds will gather but then they will disappear soon to return no more. As you progress with the Practice stillness and peace will be yours, forever.

Experiences of any nature, real as they seem at the time, do not define who you are. They are a resource for your learning. In following the Practice, with mind now quietened, you look beyond the experience. You learn what you need to learn and as the experience fades you move on, thankful, in total freedom. You are not defined by these things. So look beyond, look to the Source...

Who sees the see-er?

Who perceives the perceiver?

Who is witness to the witness?

Who is aware of the awareness?

True Self as Consciousness, an ever-present presence standing untouched by all that is experienced and felt.

* * *

True Self is not a product of the mind or of the imagination. True Self is beyond mind and imagination, ineffable, requiring no words. True Self, who you are, is for you to find as you look within, in silence and without effort...

True Self is what it is, Source, Absolute, unbounded, complete, pure and perfect.

Existence, Consciousness, Bliss. (*Sat-Chit-Ananda*)

You are This.

I Am This.

I Am I.

There is nothing more to do.

Go in peace.

Namaste.

No regret, total acceptance, nothing to forgive, no longer the seeker seeking, the controller controlling, the fixer fixing, you are free to be who you are, at peace, Love Eternal, the sun shining through the darkest cloud.

Be who you are.

Recommended Reading

Bhagavad-Gita (The Song Celestial)
Translated by Sir Edwin Arnold, Martino Publishing, 2010

Tao Te Ching
Lao Tzu, Element Books, 1997

Be As You Are – The Teachings of Sri Ramana Maharshi
Edited by David Godman, Arkana-Penguin Books, 1985

On Being You: A Simple Guide to Self Enquiry
Michael Vincent, AuthorHouse, 2010

Naked Being
JM Harrison, O-Books, 2010

The Complete Book of Zen
Wong Kiew Kit, Element Books, 1998

The Mystic Christ
Ethan Walker III, Devi Press, 2003

Wake Up and Roar
HWL Poonja, Sounds True, 2007

Teachings of the Buddha
Jack Kornfield, Shambhala, 2007

Mansur Hallaj: Life and Poems
Paul Smith, New Humanity Books, 2014

An Autobiography: The Story of My Experiments with Truth
MK Gandhi, Penguin Books, 1982

Notes

"Be true to yourself and all will go well for you."
Tao Te Ching

_____
_____
_____
_____
_____
_____
_____
_____
_____
_____
_____
_____
_____
_____
_____
_____
_____
_____
_____
_____
_____
_____
_____
_____

Notes

"But if you cannot find friend or master to go with you
Travel on alone
Like a king who has given away his kingdom
Like an elephant in the forest."
The Dhammapada

_____
_____
_____
_____
_____
_____
_____
_____
_____
_____
_____
_____
_____
_____
_____
_____
_____
_____
_____
_____
_____
_____
_____

Illustrations

Cover — Glastonbury Tor in the Autumn, Gouache, 2004

Page xii — Sea Peace, Gouache, 1995

Page 14 — Woodland Spring, Gouache, 1996

Page 20 — Moonrise over the Coromandel, NZ, Oil on canvas, 1992

Page 25 — Glastonbury Tor on a frosty morning, Gouache, 2004

Page 30 — Vermont Autumn, Gouache, 2003

Page 35 — The Somerset Levels from Butleigh Ridge, Oil on canvas, 1999

Page 39 — A walk on the Beach, Oil on canvas, 1996

Page 45 — Benacre Sunset, Oil on canvas, 1989

Page 49 — Suffolk Meadow, Oil on canvas, 1995

Page 54 — Dandelions on the Somerset Levels, Gouache, 2000

Page 60 — Benacre Sunrise, Oil on canvas, 1994

Page 65 — Contemplation: The Spirit flies, Oil on canvas, 2002/4

Page 72 — Winter Trees, Hatch Hill, Somerset, Gouache, 1998

Page 77 — Winter Trees, Gouache, 1998

Page 82 — Suffolk Dusk, Gouache, 1995

Page 88 — Earth Diva: The Spirit of Life (Detail), Oil on canvas, 2004/6

Page 93 — Primrose Yellow, Gouache, 1995

Back cover — An Incoming Tide, Gouache, 1995

About the Author

Born in Suffolk in 1949 Michael has been a painter and writer throughout his life. His inspiration is found in nature, in front of the living, vibrant landscape where painting becomes both a connection to our precious Mother Earth and an act of deep meditation.

He specialises in gouache and oil painting using reproductions of his work to illustrate his published books and articles. Several of his paintings have become limited edition prints and he has work in private collections worldwide.

In 2004 Michael was honoured to receive the Sannyasin name Tathagat from his friends at Osho Leela, a name he continues to use in his work in Self Enquiry. In 2005 he qualified as a Level 2 Reiki Practitioner (Shekinashram, Glastonbury). A lifelong interest in meditation has culminated in a deepening understanding of Self Enquiry and his first book on this simple but radical practice was published in 2010.

Michael now lives in Bridgwater, Somerset with his daughter Jennifer. From there he pursues a combined programme of creative activity and meditation taught to others through Satsang and retreats.

"I lay no claim to Divine lineage; I worship no Guru or Divinity. My understanding of the importance and profound nature of Self Enquiry has grown as life is experienced and the Practice applied in all that is presented to me. But then Self Enquiry is just This…"

For more information on Michael's work please visit:

Website: www.michaelvincentartworks.com

"My uniform experience has convinced me that there is no other God than Truth… This Truth is not only truthfulness in word but truthfulness in thought also, and not only the relative truth of our conception, but the Absolute Truth, the Eternal Principle, that is God."
Mahatma Gandhi,
An Autobiography: The Story of My Experiments with Truth, 1927

Previous Books

To Kaisa: Love, Life and Complementary Health Care
Walton Press 2001

On Being You: A Simple Guide to Self Enquiry
AuthorHouse 2010

Front and back cover illustrations and all pictures used in the book are the copyright of the author Michael Vincent.

BOOKS

O is a symbol of the world, of oneness and unity; this eye represents knowledge and insight. We publish titles on general spirituality and living a spiritual life. We aim to inform and help you on your own journey in this life.

Visit our website: http://www.o-books.com

Find us on Facebook:
https://www.facebook.com/OBooks

Follow us on Twitter: @obooks